King Arthur

Man or Myth?

Paul White

Tor Mark Press . Penryn

The Tor Mark series

Charlestown
China clay
Classic Cornish anecdotes
Classic Cornish ghost stories
Cornish fairies
Cornish fishing industry
Cornish folklore
Cornish legends
Cornish mining - at surface
Cornish mining - underground
Cornish mining industry
Cornish recipes
Cornish saints
Cornwall in camera
Cornwall's early lifeboats
Cornwall's engine houses
Cornwall's railways
Customs and superstitions
Demons, ghosts and spectres
Do you know Cornwall?
Exploring Cornwall with your car
Harry Carter - Cornish smuggler
Houses, castles and gardens
Introducing Cornwall
King Arthur - man or myth?
Lost ports of Cornwall
Old Cornwall - in pictures
The pasty book
Shipwrecks around Land's End
Shipwrecks around the Lizard
Shipwrecks around Mount's Bay
Shipwrecks - Falmouth to Looe
Shipwrecks - St Ives to Bude
South-east Cornwall
The story of Cornwall
The story of the Cornish language
The story of St Ives
The story of Truro Cathedral
Tales of the Cornish fishermen
Tales of the Cornish miners
Tales of the Cornish smugglers
Tales of the Cornish wreckers

Introduction

This book will introduce you to the evidence for the existence, or otherwise, of a historical figure born in the fifth century AD whose achievements gave rise to the legend of King Arthur. Such evidence is minimal, sketchy and ambiguous; it has to be interpreted in the light of the earliest versions of the legend, which may contain some historical facts however concealed or distorted.

Before that evidence can begin to be understood, it is also necessary to know something of the history and social conditions of the period from the late Roman period until the Saxon conquest.

Not for nothing is this period known as `the Dark Ages'. Even for the Roman period in Britain, historical information is far less abundant than you might imagine, from the cut-and-dried way it is taught in primary schools. For the period from AD 400 to AD 550 there is even less to go on. It is clear that during this time the population of Britain fell dramatically, and that it was a time of plagues, external attacks on all sides and emigration to Gaul. Yet there was a period when, for a few decades perhaps in the late fifth century and early sixth, the relentless Saxon advance was temporarily halted and even repelled in a series of battles, for which a heroic leader was surely needed. We have no historically reliable name for such a leader, but the legends give us the name Arthur.

It is in the mists of that time that we must look for a historical Arthur, a British commander-in-chief who thrust back the English: but do not expect much certainty, do not expect noble Sir Lancelot or the Lady of the Lake, and do not expect polished knights and fair damsels.

First published 1995 by Tor Mark Press,
Islington Wharf, Penryn, Cornwall TR10 8AT

ISBN 0-85025-348-9

The cover illustration, showing the coronation of Arthur, in a manuscript by Matthew Paris, is reproduced by kind permission of Chetham's Library, Manchester

Printed in Cornwall, UK, by Cornwall Litho, Redruth

The legend of Arthur

Probably, like myself, you first heard of King Arthur as a child, from a version of the stories designed for children and therefore expurgated. Most such versions are based on Arthur stories written by Sir Thomas Malory, and published by Caxton under the title *Le Morte d'Arthur.* You may even have read Malory. These stories were obviously fictional, describing a kingdom that never was; and although the children's stories may have described an ideal medieval kingdom, the Malory version is a catalogue of brutality, casual killings, rapes and incest – interspersed with a fantasy league of legendary jousters.

Most of us have also heard that in the late 1960s Arthur was proclaimed by archaeologists to be a real historical person, that he was a successful cavalry leader in the British resistance to the invading Saxons around AD 500, and that his famous Camelot was at South Cadbury just half a mile south of the A303 in Wiltshire.

This book is concerned with the historical Arthur, rather than the legendary figure, but first we need to know how the legend of Arthur was transmitted to us. Sir Thomas Malory was not its source; indeed he came at the end of a sequence of medieval storytellers who for at least 500 and probably 700 years had dealt with `the Matter of Britain', as the Arthurian legend was called. Malory reworked the French romances of his time, themselves reworkings of older materials, while himself in prison for a mixture of crimes including armed robbery, attempted murder and rape. Readers of Malory may be surprised to know that his version contains less `open manslaughter and bold bawdry' than his French originals, and that he is generally thought to have added a moral dimension.

The prime source for the earliest romances was Geoffrey of Monmouth, who around 1135 wrote a *History of the Kings of Britain*. This was one of the most popular books of the Middle Ages, popular not just in Britain but across the whole of Western Europe. A quite disproportionate part of this book concerns King Arthur, whose reign is seen as the peak of British achievements.

Geoffrey's history is largely mythical, starting with the founding of Britain by Brutus, a Trojan disposssessed by the Greeks, and including characters such as Lear and Cymbeline whose stories were later to inspire Shakespeare. As the `history' proceeds, genuine historical events are included, often half understood. We cannot tell whether Geoffrey of Monmouth believed he was telling the truth, but the important thing is that his work was widely accepted in its time as fact. Remember that there were no printed books: such evidence as was available was in manuscripts spread between libraries all across Europe, so it was next to impossible even for scholars to check facts. There was no archaeology, and only a hazy awareness of the differences between the past and the present. Geoffrey was even apparently unaware that the Romans had conquered Britain, and no contemporary drew attention to his error.

Geoffrey's lavish praise of Arthur had a major political impact. Two heirs to the throne were named Arthur, though both died young. The Normans could claim that Saxon rule had been a temporary aberration, and that they were restoring legitimacy; they particularly favoured the Welsh and Bretons. Kings of England were to use the book as a justification for invading Wales and Scotland, on the grounds that the kingdom had been united under Arthur. (Strangely, they did not consider abdicating to allow Arthur's British descendants in Cornwall and Wales to rule England.) Geoffrey's vision of Arthur's empire, his conquests and his chivalry, was to inspire Plantagenets and Tudors who believed Geoffrey of Monmouth as historical truth, and Victorian imperialists who knew it to be a powerful legend.

Geoffrey also inspired romance writers, who produced the medieval equivalent of the thriller and the bodice-ripper. Breton and French authors in particular seized upon his work, and used their vivid imaginations to build from the bare bones of the Arthur story, interleaved with other stories from folklore, the equivalent of historical novels. As each generation of romancers built upon their predecessors' work, they added new characters including Lancelot and Galahad and introduced wondrous happenings such as the sword in the stone, the Round Table and the whole of the Grail Quest. Stories originally quite independent of King Arthur were relocated in his court, such as the Cornish love story of Tristan and Iseult. Each writer added his or her own sense of morality, and sometimes an appreciation of courtly love and chivalrous behaviour which was quite alien to Geoffrey.

There was and is no single 'correct' way of telling these tales: every age, and every author, is free to create their own Arthurian court. The tales were the equivalent of Westerns: figures believed to be historical (King Mark or Billy the Kid) can be intermingled with the purely fictional. Even when a character in a Western is `real', we do not expect the story to be historically reliable. The same was true for the Arthur stories.

The development of the legendary Arthur is fascinating in its own right, but is not within the scope of this book. We shall need to look at the story told by Geoffrey of Monmouth, recognise its difference from the Arthur we are used to, and then consider what Geoffrey's sources may have been and whether there are other sources of which Geoffrey was unaware.

Modern views of the historical Arthur

Where Geoffrey of Monmouth was the single prime source for the legendary Arthur, there are three writers who have particularly shaped present-day views of the `historical' Arthur, the Dark Age warrior: Geoffrey Ashe (*The Quest for Arthur's Britain*, 1968), Professor Leslie Alcock (*Arthur's Britain*, 1971) and Dr John Morris (*The Age of Arthur*, 1973).

The first two books present the archaeological and literary evidence carefully and they can both be recommended but the reader should know that, in the light of later evidence and academic discussion, both authors have since first publication retracted or seriously changed their views.

The late Dr Morris's book, reissued in paperback in 1993 and in consequence readily available, is alas rather tragic: a warning is needed because those who read it may think they understand the history of Dark Age Britain and Ireland. As one reviewer said, `It is a matter of deep regret that such an outwardly impressive piece of scholarship should crumble upon inspection into a tangled tissue of fact and fantasy which is both misleading and misguided.'

Arthurian studies have a fascination which can take hold of a person and drive them to distraction. Authors who seek `to offer the first historical proof of the existence of King Arthur' will almost invariably make fools of themselves, and there have been many other books written since the 1960s which have claimed to solve the mystery. At the root of the problem lies the shortage of direct evidence even of Arthur's existence. And a further problem is that each piece of evidence lies in a different field of scholarship: archaeology, various aspects of history, Celtic studies, philology, place names. No single scholar is competent to assess the evidence in all of these areas, so none dares try. It is left to us amateurs.

Another problem lies in the ambiguity of the sources. If a medieval writer refers to *Britannia*, he might mean the island of Britain, or that part of the island under British control, or Brittany, or the British people. The same ambiguity extends to Dumnonia, Cornovia, or `King Mark'. Confusion is inevitable; frequently our source itself seems uncertain.

Proving the existence of Arthur is like proving the existence of God: in either case it is impossible to convince a sceptic, however convincing the arguments might be for fellow believers. In the case of Arthur, every such writer comes up with a quite different `proven truth'! Some find Arthur in the West Country, some in Scotland; one recent Arthur is from Gwynedd but based himself in Wroxeter. Some are minor local kings, some are just tribal war-leaders; some operate in a narrow area of country, others are high kings of Britain. Dr Morris's Arthur was 'the last Emperor of the West' and bore a striking resemblance to Winston Churchill.

What are we to make of it all? Firstly, that many authors are on an ego-trip and see themselves as Sherlock Holmes; and secondly that their publishers want a novelty solution to the riddle of Arthur.

This book is not written under that kind of pressure, but rather in the hope that readers are grown-up enough to accept that there is no ultimate proof – but that the fascination lies in the trail.

Geoffrey of Monmouth's version

Geoffrey was presumably born in Monmouth but his family may have been Breton by origin, possibly one of many Breton families who came over at the Norman Conquest. The Bretons are descended from the British who emigrated in the fifth and sixth centuries, while the Saxons were conquering Britain. He may have spoken Breton, possibly Welsh, probably enough English to demand a jug of ale, and certainly Norman French, but he spent most of his life at Oxford as a scholar, and he wrote in Latin. Naturally like all scholars he was in holy orders, and was made Bishop of St Asaph in Wales late in his life; it is thought he never went there. Geoffrey has no doubt that Arthur was conceived at Tintagel.

The story so far: King Uther has just pacified the northern peoples with the exemplary ferocity which Geoffrey calls justice. Now read on.

> The festival of Easter was approaching so Uther commanded the barons of his kingdom to meet in London so that he could celebrate the important day with honour, wearing the crown of state. All and sundry made themselves ready and arrived in time for the festival. So the King celebrated the festival as he had intended, and enjoyed himself along with his barons, who rejoiced that he had welcomed them so cheerfully. For indeed

the nobles had all brought their wives and daughters, as was appropriate for such an occasion.

Among them was Gorlois Duke of Cornwall with his wife Ingerna, whose beauty exceeded that of the other British women. When Uther noticed her among the throng, he totally ignored all the other women and concentrated his entire attention upon her. To her alone he kept instructing the servants to take the best dishes; and using his close associates as go-betweens he sent her gold cups for the toast. He laughed and joked with her on many occasions. Her husband saw precisely what was happening; he was immediately angry and withdrew from court without asking permission from the King. No one could persuade him to return, because he was afraid he would lose the one thing he prized above all. Uther in turn was angry, and commanded him to return to court to face punishment for insulting him. When it was clear that Gorlois had fled, Uther swore with solemn oaths that he would ravage Gorlois's land unless he hurried back to give satisfaction.

A deadline was fixed, and passed, and the quarrel remained. Uther took an army to Cornwall and set fire to towns and strongholds. Gorlois did not dare to meet him in the field, being outnumbered, so he prepared to sit out a siege in his strongholds until he could get help from Ireland; since he was more concerned for his wife than for himself, he put her in the stronghold of Tintagel, by the seashore, which he believed to be the safer refuge. He himself entered Castle Dimilioc so that if a disaster occurred they would not both be endangered simultaneously.

When the King learned of this, he went to the stronghold in which Gorlois was, and besieged it, cutting off all access. Remembering the torments of love for Ingerna through which he had passed, Uther called on Ulfin Ridcaradoch, a friend and fellow warrior, and told him in these words what troubled him: `I am burning with love for Ingerna, and I am sure I shall become seriously ill if I don't have her. You must advise me how I can fulfil my desire, or I shall die of the torment.'

Ulfin replied, `Who can give you any advice that will work, when there is no way of forcing an access to her in the stronghold of Tintagel? For it is in the sea, and inaccessible on all sides from the sea, and there is no other entry except by a narrow rock. It could be protected by three armed soldiers even if you threw the whole army of Britain against it. On the other hand, if the prophet Merlin were prepared to get involved, I imagine you could get your way with his help.'

Believing this, the king had Merlin summoned, for he was present at the siege. When he was in the presence of the King, he was ordered to advise how the king could fulfil his desire for Ingerna. He observed the strength of the King's torment, and was moved by the sight of such a great love. He said, `To get your desire, new arts will have to be used which are unheard of in the age you live in. I can by the use of drugs give you the appearance of Gorlois, so that in every respect you will be seen as him. If you agree to this, I shall make you absolutely like him, and I shall turn Ulfin into Jordanus of Tintagel, his close friend. I shall join you in a third disguise, and you can go to the castle and get access to Ingerna.'

The King agreed, and concentrated on what Merlin said. Then he delegated command of the siege, took the drugs Merlin gave him, and was transformed into Gorlois. At the same time, Ulfin was changed into Jordanus and Merlin into Britahelm, so well that no one could have told the difference. Then they set out for Tintagel and arrived at dusk at the stronghold. The gatekeeper was certain that his lord had arrived, so the gates were opened and the men admitted. What else could happen, when it was quite obvious that Gorlois stood there? The king spent the night with Ingerna and refreshed himself with the love he had desired, for he deceived her too by his false appearance and by the artful explanation which he gave. He said he had stolen away from the siege especially to check that his beloved was well, and the stronghold secure. And she believed everything he said. That very same night, renowned Arthur was conceived, who through his great worth deserved the fame he has received.

What would the tabloid press give now for such a royal story?

`Castle Dimilioc' was the hill-fort now occupied by the church of St Dennis in the china clay country. Until recently it was possible to dismiss Tintagel as the location for whatever actual event (if any) may have given rise to this story, since Tintagel had been a Celtic monastery at the time. It was assumed that Geoffrey had located the story at Tintagel because his patron the Earl of Cornwall had just begun building his castle there, and Geoffrey had wanted to please him by associating the Earl's castle with the famous hero. But the excavations at Tintagel in 1990-1 showed that the site was never a monastery, and was indeed used in the fifth and sixth centuries as a stronghold, possibly on a seasonal basis since it would be all but uninhabitable in winter storms. Moreover, it was discovered that the medieval castle was not started until a century after Geoffrey was writing, so there was no reason at all to name Tintagel unless there was a tradition already in existence.

Geoffrey's story continues. While Uther was having his wicked way, Dimiliock fell and Gorlois is dead. There has been `outrageous plundering'; but what was outrageous was that the attackers just grabbed what came their way rather than drawing lots for their share. A messenger comes to inform Ingerna of Gorlois's death, but Uther is still in the guise of Gorlois. He has to pretend it's a false rumour, but worrying. He goes away as Gorlois to check, and returns as King Uther to claim his bride.

On Uther's death, Arthur is chosen as king at the age of fifteen. Large numbers of warriors flock to him; honour demands that he should give each of them a gift, and in his youthful generosity he overspends. The treasury is empty, so he decides to raid the Saxons for loot, aided by his Breton nephew Hoel. Arthur then fights first Saxons, then Scots (i.e. Irish), then Picts in battles ranging from Lincolnshire to Loch Lomond. Then he conquers Ireland. Not surprisingly some neighbouring kings voluntarily submit themselves, but Arthur still has to conquer Norway, Denmark and a substantial part of Gaul. He grants Normandy to his `butler' Beduerus (Sir Bedivere) and Anjou to his `steward' Kaius (Sir Kay).

There follows a war on the continent against the Romans, in which there is much smiting and cleaving of helms and not a little success. But back in Britain Mordred (acting as regent in Arthur's absence) rebels, and invites the Saxons, Picts and Scots to help him. Arthur returns, chases Mordred around the country and finally to Cornwall, where in a battle on the River Camel Mordred is killed and many thousands with him.

> But the famous King Arthur was himself fatally wounded; he was carried away to the Isle of Avalon and passed on his crown to his relative Constantine, son of Cador Duke of Cornwall, in the year 542 AD. May his soul rest in peace.

Before we look at the sources Geoffrey may have used for his history, and whether they can be relied upon, let us first consider what is known about late Roman Britain, the departure of the Romans, and the arrival of the Saxons – the period often called `the Dark Ages' because of the lack of reliable evidence.

Late Roman Britain

Roman Britain did not cease to exist one midnight in AD 410. There was in fact no single `departure of the Romans'. Roman army units had been leaving Britain for many years; they were not `recalled to defend mainland Europe', as we used to be taught in school, but were led abroad by ambitious generals to fight civil wars in pursuit of the imperial throne.

The civil government remained, until it was deposed in a minor but bloody revolution in 408 or 409. This revolution brought new people to power, but there was never an official break with Rome, and Romano-British civilized life was at first little changed, although contact with Rome was lost because northern Gaul had been over-run by `barbarians'. It is conjectured that Arthur was a very late `Romano-Briton', bilingual in British and Latin and with a broadly classical education, and using military methods of the late Roman period. So to understand Arthur, we need to understand something of the social and political history of the century before his birth, during which Britain went through a great period of change. But if you want to avoid a history lesson, you could skip to the next mention of Arthur on page 16!

At the end of the fourth century, Britain had been part of the Roman Empire for well over 300 years. What did this mean?

It is normal to make a broad distinction between the lowland and upland zones: the `upland zone' included the south-west peninsula, the whole of Wales, the Pennine uplands and all of Scotland south of the Clyde-Forth line. (Hadrian's Wall was not the boundary of the Empire but a defensible fall-back line, well behind the frontier.) The upland zone remained far less `Romanised' than the lowlands; population density was thinner, towns were further apart, smaller and with fewer facilities, agriculture and trade were less developed, and probably the older Celtic tribal ways were still dominant. The army was a significant factor in these areas, which were still frontier territory, raided by the Picts from the highlands of Scotland and the `Scotti' or Irish from across the sea.

Lowland Britain, on the other hand, was a crucial and integrated part of the Empire. Its population had grown greatly: the total population of Britain may have been as many as six million in AD 200, and much of the land was developed for agriculture, though some of it was later abandoned. Industries were active, especially factories supplying pottery, clothing and armour to the armed forces.

Britannia was divided into four (and for a time five) provinces, each with a governor and a substantial civil service. Above them, and based in London, was the *vicarius* or governor of the whole `diocese'. The main administrative unit was the *civitas* (plural *civitates*), of which there were perhaps 28. These had been based on the pre-Roman tribes, but the growth of population had led to subdivisions. Devon and Cornwall formed the civitas of Dumnonia. The civitas usually had a capital city, which became synonymous with the civitas: Dumnonia was governed from Isca Dumnoniorum, Isca of the Dumnonians, now Exeter.

The Empire was vast, and held together uncertainly. Officially there were at any time not one but four emperors; both the Western Empire and the Eastern Empire had a senior emperor, the Augustus, and a junior emperor, the Caesar. The government of Britain was responsible not to Rome, but to Trier in Germany. But in practice disputes between the official emperors, and attempts by army commanders to promote themselves, could lead to extensive civil wars with as many as seven or eight imperial claimants leading armies against each other around mainland Europe. Because Britain had a large part of the standing army, a number of these claimants had come from Britain. Britain had been outside the Roman Empire at least twice as a result of these rebellions.

The Empire had successfully eliminated pro-Italian prejudice, and the emperors themselves were usually not Italian. All free men were citizens of the Empire, and could move freely between countries, aided by the Latin language universally spoken among the administrators, army and merchants, as well as among all well-to-do households and their servants. In Britain the Celtic language survived in the lowland area among the lower class (the vast majority of the population) and possibly more generally in the upland zone. This `Brythonic' language was the predecessor of Welsh, Cornish and Breton, but it had case endings like Latin. It was absorbing many Latin words (of which there are several hundred in modern Welsh) and it was a `cousin' of the early Irish `Goidelic' language.

Each civitas had its own *curia* or council with about a hundred members. This was not an elected body, but depended on the local aristocracy and their sense of duty to the state. These people could be very rich indeed, and they usually had a town house and a country villa on their estate. The people who farmed the estates were mostly tied to the land, like later serfs, and a minority were slaves in the sense that they could be bought and sold. The lifestyle of the landowning class was a round of hunting, house parties and the cultivation of the arts. It would not be unreasonable to compare this society with the Russia of Tolstoy's novels.

The growth of external attacks from barbarians who envied this rich lifestyle had to be parried by greater military force, which led to increasing government costs, which were met by ruthlessly increased central taxation. But the rich were able to avoid taxation, as were the civil servants, the army and the increasingly influential and often wealthy Christian priests. A larger tax burden and a smaller tax base meant that the poor and the middle class were squeezed. There is evidence of rural depopulation, presumably the result of starvation, and of recession in the economy of many towns, for a century before AD 410.

More and more of the economy fell into the hands of the richest magnates, and more still into the hands of the Emperor, not least because the numerous rebellions led to confiscation of estates. The Emperor also owned most of the factories. It was a centrally controlled economy, nothing like modern western capitalism.

What religions did these people practise? The official religion of the Empire was Christianity; it had been adopted as a means of state control and was the natural religion for anyone who wanted to get on in the world. It had totally lost any subversive or slave-class image it may have had 250 years earlier. So far from persecuting Christians, the emperors had begun to persecute other religions, particularly under the influence of Ambrosius of Milan. Their targets included the various traditional religions of classical Rome. People might practise several religions at once, not seeing any conflict between them: the old state religion (Jove, Mercury, Venus etc) was mainly a matter of social form, the various mystery religions such as Mithraism and the worship of Osiris provided a more intense experience, and the worship of the `household gods' was for most families a deeply-rooted obligation.

Many of the most respectable and moral people of the time were deeply shocked and resentful of Christian intolerance. A rebellion in Britain in 392-4 appears to have been an anti-Christian backlash, although its leader Eugenius was himself a Christian. Indeed British Christians seem to have sought a more socially just form of Christianity even before contact with the Empire was lost.

In the countryside the pagani or country-folk still continued to worship the old Celtic gods, which had often assimilated the characteristics of Roman nature-worship. Unfortunately history is written by the victors, and the victors in this case were the Christian monks, who insultingly lumped together all other religions as `pagan' – meaning `peasant'. We know all too little about them. And yet there is surprisingly little evidence of Christian worship in late Roman Britain, except in the richest villas, and rather more evidence of the continuing worship of Celtic gods such as Nodens. For the majority of the population Christianity at this time would have seemed a rich man's religion, whose bishops and priests lived in high style at state expense.

Civilians in the Empire were forbidden to carry arms; they generally did not need them, because there was little lawlessness. However it is clear that some of the attacks by the Picts, the Scots and later the `Saxons' (a general term for people from across the North Sea) caused severe problems for the defence of Britain. The regular army was much smaller than one might imagine, only around 6000 men, to cover attacks which might occur along the Lancashire coast, the Yorkshire coast, the Wall and the whole of East Anglia. There was a considerable Irish settlement in what is now Dyfed and for many in Wales, Lancashire or Cornwall the Irish raiders were a more serious danger than the Saxons.

The general policy of the Empire was to settle one militarily vigorous barbarian tribe on its border to hold off other possible attackers, paying them first with land and later with gold. Such settlers were called federates. It may be that some Saxons were settled in Eastern England in this way before 400. There is evidence that towns provided themselves with walls and improved fortifications at this time, including artillery platforms, and it is possible they employed Saxon troops. Certainly the legions included many `Saxons' serving under `Roman' officers. Britain at that time was a multi-ethnic, multicultural and multilingual society. A tombstone found in South Shields commemorating a woman named Regina, a slave who was from the Catuvellauni tribe in southern Britain, was set up by her husband, a dealer in military flags from Palmyra in Syria. The tombstone is carved in Latin and Palmyrene, but not in British since at that time no one had worked out how to write it down.

What happened after AD 400?

The honest answer is we do not know! Our information about the Roman period is far less certain than we might expect but it is full indeed compared to our knowledge of the period from 400 to 600, when there are few good written sources and fragmentary archaeological evidence. The following account is one version of what may have happened, in which every statement and every date is controversial!

In AD395, after the suppression of the revolt of Eugenius, Britain seemed as stable a part of the Empire as any and yet by 402 the Emperor Honorius had ceased to make payments to his army and civil service in Britain. We know this because the coin sequence stops, and before long Britain had ceased to have a money economy but returned to barter. The emperor may have been unable to afford to pay, or unable to transfer the cash because of piracy.

The army in Britain was soon preparing itself against attack from the continent, either by the Germans who had virtually over-run Gaul (and were to cut Britain off from the rest of the Roman world) or perhaps from an opposing Roman army. In 407, a general who had proclaimed himself Emperor Constantine III invaded Gaul from Britain, successfully taking back large areas from the Germans. This could have been seen as reclaiming land for the empire but inevitably he became involved in imperial politics and in wars against Honorius himself, which he ultimately lost. All these `Roman' armies consisted of barbarian mercenaries, many of them German.

In 408, while Britain was denuded of troops, there were further Saxon raids. In desperation the Britons rebelled against the absent imperial claimant, Constantine, and set up their own administration. At that time no one in Britain or Rome imagined this was the end of Roman rule. The Britons expelled or executed the `Romans', who were probably mainly Gallo-Roman aristocrats since there were not many really powerful Britons. Army units were disbanded or given land instead of pay. For decades Britain had been backing new imperial claimants from among their army commanders in the hope that they would improve the system of government; now, for the first time, the Britons had questioned the whole corrupt and incompetent system.

The Emperor Honorius approved of Britain rebelling against Constantine (who was by now his bitter enemy) and was in no position to intervene. He therefore wrote to the 28 civitates (significantly not to the governors of the provinces) telling them to defend themselves as best they could. This was in 410. Much to everyone's surprise, they did! The Saxons were pushed back and there appears to have been a period of great prosperity following the end of

Roman rule. A little caution is necessary, however: our main source for this prosperity is the monk Gildas, writing over a century later. Not only is his knowledge of the history of this period demonstrably shaky, but he may have had a class bias. It is quite possible that the rich British landowners benefited, for example from the confiscation of foreign-owned estates, as well as from even lower taxation and from the disbanding of an army which frequently took their best farm labourers as conscripts. Whether this prosperity `trickled down' is another matter. Most probably only the rich benefited, the poor were no worse off, and the main casualties were the middle classes: with the virtual end of trade, certainly the end of a money economy, town life declined. Some towns such as Wroxeter and St Albans certainly continued for another hundred years, albeit with wooden rather than masonry buildings; probably they became administrative and military centres with little commercial activity.

It is also possible that the prosperity did not extend to the north and west, where Irish and Pictish invasions continued. At least one of these raids led to the abandonment of northern towns, followed by guerrilla warfare against the invaders which was finally successful.

The leaders of the civitates gradually took on the character of local kings. There was some kind of council at which one king, Vortigern, possibly from mid-Wales, acquired a wider control. He invited a group of Saxons under Hengist and Horsa to settle in Kent as federates, giving them land in Thanet in return for military service. Perhaps he wanted them there to deter an imperial invasion. He did not consult the 'king' of Kent before he acted.

Vortigern was opposed by another Briton, named Ambrosius. It is possible that their disputes were personal, or tribal, or that Ambrosius represented a pro-Roman (pro-European!) party and Vortigern a `nationalist' party; or there may have been a religious element since by this time many Britons were `Pelagians'. Pelagius was a Briton who had suggested that people had freewill to behave well or badly; in Rome this was declared heretical, the view of Augustine that sin was inevitable being preferred – a foreshadowing of the arguments of the Reformation. One of the more reliable pieces of evidence for the period concerns the visit to Britain in 429 by Bishop Germanus of Auxerre, a bishop with a military background, whose mission was to crush this heresy. He found a Romanised state functioning normally, although there was plenty with which to disagree doctrinally.

Some time in the late 440s, the Saxon federates rebelled. There was a period of destruction and looting, and a famine. The British appealed to the commander of the Roman armies in Gaul, Aëtius, but he ignored `the groans of the Britons'. Vortigern and his son Vortipor struggled to drive back the Saxons. They were deposed, however in favour of Ambrosius Aurelianus, who was perhaps a son of the Ambrosius who had earlier opposed Vortigern. He is one of very few historical figures to be named by Gildas (see below), who says Ambrosius was perhaps the last of the Romans to survive and that his parents had `undoubtedly worn the purple' but had been killed in the Saxon uprising. (This phrase about wearing the purple is extremely ambiguous, since *parentes* can poetically mean grandparents or even ancestors, as well as parents. And whilst wearing the purple was a prerogative of emperors, people of senatorial rank wore a toga with a broad purple stripe.) Whatever his antecedents, Ambrosius Aurelianus was clearly able to rally the Britons, who then held and partially forced back the Saxons. Warfare continued indecisively for many years.

In 468 a mysterious but undoubtedly historical character called Riothamos, `King of the Britons', led a large British army into Gaul via Brittany, to fight on the side of the Emperor against the Visigoths. Initially he was victorious but before he could link his army with the Emperor's he was defeated, possibly through treachery, and faded from history near the town of Avallon in Burgundy. Riothamus was not a name but a title – something like `chief king'. What was his personal name? Could *he* have been Arthur?

Already by this time there was a substantial British presence in Brittany. Some of these immigrants were the survivors of earlier expeditionary forces, some were probably there as federates to oppose the Saxon raids. Many were emigrants fleeing the wars, plagues and famines of Britain. They found Brittany much depopulated, and either bought or just occupied the land. They appear to have migrated and settled in large, well-organised groups, led by religious leaders and even by local kings, and from the evidence of Breton place names they appear to have left mainly from the southwest of England.

In Britain, the war against the Saxons continued under Ambrosius Aurelianus' successor and a series of battles against Saxon enemies and against the Picts and Scots culminated around AD 500 in a great victory at the siege of Badon Hill, which probably overlooked the city of Bath. The victor of these battles was Arthur, who then enjoyed some years of peace before a civil war broke out in which Arthur died, at the Battle of Camlann around 516. The Saxons remained subdued for another fifty years: indeed they seem to have begun migrating back to the Continent. The

Britons at peace were more disunited than ever and minor wars between the British kingdoms were normal throughout the century, even as the Saxons conquered them one by one. But the Saxons too were by no means united, and they too fought each other.

When the Saxons of Wessex took the offensive in the 550s (ironically under Cynric whose name suggests he was British) there was no Arthur to unite the Britons and following the Battle of Dyrham in 577 the Saxons reached the Bristol Channel, finally dividing the Britons of Dumnonia (the south-west) from the Britons of Wales. They had taken the most productive lowland areas and left the Britons with the harsher land. `England' as we know it existed by AD 600, leaving British kingdoms in Dumnonia and Wales, and in central Scotland. The population of southern and western England, and probably of much of eastern England too, remained predominantly British, but accepted the language, culture and laws of the victors.

It must be restated that the account above is not merely highly simplified, but that nearly every statement made is controversial because the evidence is either minimal or ambiguous.

The evidence

What are we looking for? Firstly evidence of what happened politically or militarily, and when. By what stages did the Saxons acquire power and territory from the Britons – and from which areas did the Britons emigrate, or die of plagues; were the Britons `ethnically cleansed' or assimilated into `English' society? Did the Saxons arrive in force and occupy the land, or in comparatively small numbers but as conquerors, as did the Normans later?

Secondly we seek some understanding of the stages by which a wealthy Romanized country of six million people turned into a mass of warring miniature kingdoms, both British and Saxon, of considerable poverty both material and cultural, and a total population of about one million. Did wars or plagues, emigration or famine, cause such a drop in the population?

And thirdly we would like to know something about Arthur.

Perhaps in the light of the disappearance of the Soviet bloc and the collapsed economies and near starvation of the people of Ukraine and Georgia, we have an example of what the end of a great empire might be like; the Roman Empire too was a centralised economy. Could the wars in Arthur's Britain have been something like Bosnia in the 1990s? Such comparisons may remind us of the scale of great national disasters, but is the evidence there for Britain in the fifth century? What we can say is that it was a period of turbulent change, that plagues, famines and wars certainly took a toll of many individuals, and that many emigrated deliberately or in desperation and gave their name and language to Brittany, a nation which in its turn now struggles for cultural survival having long since lost its independence.

There is no space here to give all the evidence relating to this period or even a small part. Some is archaeological but that gives us no names. Some evidence is written, and referred to as `sources'. To be reliable, a source needs to have been written shortly after the events it describes, by someone whose attitudes and prejudices can be assessed, and must be unambiguous in its statements and have been accurately transmitted from that time to this. No source for this period meets any of these criteria.

Gildas and Bede

The nearest approximation is the monk Gildas, who wrote a diatribe against the evil ways of his times, and particularly the wickedness of five British kings. Gildas was a patriotic Romano-Briton who thought in Latin and wrote it quite well in a classical rather than monkish style. Unfortunately his most important statements for our purposes tend also to be his most ambiguous! He appears to say (but it can be disputed) that he was born in the year of the battle of Mount Badon, and is now 44 years old. But as we can date neither Badon nor Gildas reliably to within 30 years, we cannot use either to date the other.

Gildas was not writing a history, but an extended sermon: his literary model was the prophet Jeremiah. He covered briefly the history of the previous two centuries as a way of pointing out past errors which were being repeated (for example rebelliousness) and past virtues which had been lost. He was wildly wrong in many of his facts (for example believing Hadrian's Wall to have been constructed around AD 395) and laments the lack of records: they must, he says, have been taken to Brittany during the period of emigration, and in this he may be correct. He can be presumed to be increasingly accurate as he approaches his own time, since his audience had sufficient knowledge of recent events to be aware of any serious blunders.

Despite the fact that, if Arthur existed, he must have been alive until Gildas was a young man, Gildas does not mention him. But then he mentions very few names other than Ambrosius Aurelianus and the evil kings who ruled when he was writing. He does not even name Vortigern. He mentions the siege of Mount

Badon, but not the name of the British general, nor any details of the battle. We do not even know who besieged whom.

The justifiably famous historian Bede, writing around 730, used Gildas as his main source for this period, although he must have had another source since he gives us the name Vortigern where Gildas referred only to a *superbus tyrannus* – another phrase of irritating ambiguity. *Superbus* means proud, arrogant or else magnificent. *Tyrannus* means a king, but it is not the usual word which is *rex*. A *tyrannus* is either a despot or a usurper. Gildas refers to five British kings of his own time, all of them *tyranni.* Since the name Vortigern was originally a title (like Riothamus) meaning high king, it has even been suggested that Gildas is playing on Vortigern's name, which might translate into Latin as *superbus tyrannus*. This is just one example among thousands of the difficulties faced by translators, even from a well-documented language like Latin, which can greatly affect our understanding of the period when there are so few other sources to cross-check against. Bede also does not mention Arthur by name.

Chronicles and Annals

The Anglo-Saxon Chronicle is a very unreliable source for the early years of the Saxons in Britain, since it was compiled much later, and in any case omits all mention of Saxon set-backs. There are other annals, none of them totally reliable however, from Gaul and Ireland which offer clues to dating and there is also a set of `Welsh Annals'. It should be remembered that none of these sources survive in original manuscripts. They have been copied many times, with accidental errors in copying and often deliberate editing. Later copyists may have added material from other sources if they thought it interesting, or have deliberately falsified the text if it helped their monastery's pretensions. Scholars argue endlessly over what can or cannot be relied upon!

The Welsh Annals tell us (in Latin):

501 Battle of Badon in which Arthur carried the cross of Our Lord Jesus Christ for three days and nights on his shoulders and the Britons were victors.

537 Battle of Camlann in which Arthur and Medraut fell and there was a plague in Britain and Ireland.

It is not even clear whether Arthur and Medraut were on opposite sides or the same side.

Nennius

Another Welsh source probably dating in part from around 830 is known as `Nennius', the name of its supposed author. Called *The History of the Britons* and written in indifferent monkish Latin, this gives an extended version of the arrival of the Saxons but is brief about Arthur, listing the names of twelve battles. These place names cannot be positively identified, though there are many modern books which claim otherwise! They appear to range from Lincolnshire to Loch Lomond and imply a variety of enemies. `Nennius' is an unreliable source, but very tempting to anyone trying to write a history of the period, because other sources are lacking. Certainly Geoffrey of Monmouth used it.

Like the rest of our sources, Nennius can be maddeningly unhelpful. It tells us 'Then Arthur fought with them in those days', but omits to tell us who 'they' were, or in what days! Arthur was fighting *cum regibus Brittonum sed ipse dux erat bellorum,* 'with the kings of the Britons but he was himself the leader in battle'. This last phrase has been endlessly debated by scholars. Clearly Arthur was commander in chief, but does it mean he was not a king himself? Or was he a king among others, but trusted with the job of leading the combined armies? The phrase *dux bellorum* literally means 'leader of wars' but may represent a formal title. The word *dux* means either leader or general, or 'The Leader' as in Mussolini, 'il Duce'. It gave us our word 'Duke' and the Venetians their 'Doge'; in the fourth century there had been a *Dux Britanniarum,* who commanded the army of Hadrians Wall. It is alas impossible to know which interpretation to make.

Nennius tells us that at the battle of Badon Hill 'in a single day 960 men fell from a single charge by Arthur, and no one laid them low except he himself.' Those who wish to disparage Nennius regard the claim as an example of his credulity, but it probably means that Arthur's army was on this occasion acting without the assistance of the other kings of Britain, and so deserved even greater credit for the victory.

Welsh poetry

If the historical writers are obscure and imprecise, the poets are even more so! Early Welsh poets prided themselves on allusion and subtle references which the most knowledgeable and astute in their audience might appreciate, and their verse forms, especially the formal englyn which is still used by modern Welsh poets, are formidably difficult to write and thrive on ambiguity.

There are two ancient poems, both of which may date from as early as the sixth century, which mention Arthur in passing. These poems were produced by bards at British courts to sing the praises of the ruler, his ancestors, and their war-bands. The war-band consisted of warriors not just from that kingdom or tribe, but from all over the country, rather like a modern soccer team. There was much feasting and drinking and mutual present-giving; the bards were well paid for describing scenes of battle and of feasting in a way that brought honour to the king and his family.

The earliest surviving poems were probably produced in northern Britain (southern Scotland today) among the tribe known in Latin as the Votadini, and in Welsh as the Gododdin, and also in the kingdom of Rheged with its capital at Carlisle. A famous poem composed around 600 by Aneirin describes a raid from Edinburgh against the Saxon kingdom of Deira; a battle takes place at Catterick, in which the Gododdin war-band is wiped out – but heroically! One warrior in this poem

> glutted the ravens on the wall of the fort
> though he was not Arthur.

`Arthur' was clearly the name of a famous hero, known possibly to the poet but possibly to a later bard who recited the poem, or to the person who first committed it to paper, generations later.

Another poem about the death of Geraint of Dumnonia at the Battle of Llongborth (which may have been Langport in Somerset, on the then border of Dumnonia, or Portchester the Roman fort on Southampton Water) has a reference of great ambiguity, which apparently may be literally translated:

> In Llongborth [or `In a naval port'] I saw Arthur's
> brave men - (they) used to slay with steel -
> the emperor, the leader (in the) toil (of battle).

It is unclear whether Arthur was at this battle or whether there was a band known as `Arthur's men'. Again the manuscript is much later than the poem; and the poem is in Welsh, not British, as it would have been if written shortly after the events it describes. British went through a rapid period of change into early Welsh in the sixth and seventh centuries. Since the change involved the loss of case endings, it is argued that older poems would have become obsolete because the metre would have been destroyed.

The Geraint for whom the elegy was written was almost certainly from the Dumnonian royal house, so this is an early if vague connection of Arthur and Cornwall.

Another Welsh poem about the graves of famous men has a reference to Arthur's grave, '*anoeth* is a grave for Arthur'. *Anoeth* is a very rare word, meaning something like a hopeless quest or wild goose chase.

In *The dialogue of Arthur and the Eagle*, Arthur is an aristocrat, a religiously uneducated but sympathetic pagan, who receives Christian instruction from an eagle. Arthur here is not a king, but a war-leader, and two interesting phrases are used about him. He is *Arth llu* or 'bear of the host' which has made some people suppose the name Arthur was not Artorius, but a nickname 'Bear'. And he is *pen kadoed Kernyw*, 'head of the hosts of Cornwall', where the word for 'hosts' is the same as the word for 'battles', so this phrase might translate into Latin as *dux bellorum*.

Saints' Lives

Much of the literary production of the early medieval period consisted of `Lives' of the saints, particularly of the patron saint of the monastery of the writer. These are not biographies as we understand the term, but naive attempts to aggrandise the saint (and indirectly the monastery) with accounts of miracles and successful confrontations with temporal rulers. In Welsh 'Lives', Arthur makes a number of appearances; he frequently cuts an unheroic figure and is often a figure of fun or even hatred, for example as a *tyrannus* who commandeers church property which the saint forces him to restore. Arthur's centre of operations is generally Dumnonia, and in particular 'Kelliwic' in Cornwall – which has been tentatively identified with a hill fort near Wadebridge. In one instance he is only a joint king in Somerset.

A Welsh life of St Gildas, written in the twelfth century, makes Gildas and Arthur contemporaries, which is by no means impossible although Arthur would have been somewhat older, and shows them not at all friendly to each other. Gildas mediates when the king of Somerset, Melwas, has abducted Guinevere and is holding her in the fort at Glastonbury; Gildas persuades Melwas to release her before he is attacked by Arthur, who has brought levies from Devon and Cornwall.

All such stories are unreliable; they were never intended as historical truth. At most they give us hints. They suggest that Arthur might not have been universally admired, and in particular not by the monks. He may have been known to Gildas, but a family or political enemy, which could explain why Gildas does not name him. Could the Celtic church have been embarassed by a national hero who was himself not a Christian (as in *The Dialogue of Arthur and the Eagle*) or of a diferent ideology? Or did he finance his wars by raiding church funds? Or perhaps he was remembered in the upland areas of Wales as an arrogant lowlander who expected everyone to stump up taxes for wars which they judged too distant to matter?

We cannot know, but ironically this adverse view of a national hero makes it *more* likely that a historical Arthur existed; leaders who succeed in bringing about great changes do not attract universal admiration and indeed will be thought by some contemporaries to have caused more damage than good – a Margaret Thatcher or a Lenin is likely to create a few enemies.

Saints' *Lives* were not confined to Wales; the Breton *Life of St Goeznovius* draws on a different tradition from the Welsh. In this Arthur is `the great king of the Britons' who stemmed the advance of the Saxons, winning victories in Britain and Gaul. This both recalls `Riothamus' and suggests that the Breton (and probably also Cornish) traditions of Arthur, rather than the Welsh, were the sources of Geoffrey of Monmouth's history. Virtually nothing survives of medieval Breton or Cornish literature of any kind, so the Breton tradition remains unknown. However, it is likely that it was the Breton tradition which inspired the earliest French romances.

Other Welsh references

Welsh secular storytellers and poets had innumerable tales of Arthur, some of which have survived. He is often associated with Cei, Bedwyr and Gwalchmei (known to us as Sir Kay, Sir Bedivere and Sir Gawain) and takes part in fantastic quests and hunts for magic beasts. The bards had a technique for memorising the themes of stories in `triads'; these were artificial groupings of three, for example `The three wicked uncoverings' or `The three red ravagers'. Tantalisingly the lists survive, but not the stories themselves, though sometimes a brief outline remains. One of the wicked uncoverings was when Arthur dug up the head of the god Bran, which had been buried on Tower Hill in London, because he did not wish to rely on its magical protection. Another tells us that Arthur had no less than three wives each called Guinevere. It is fascinating folklore, but of limited help in the search for a historical Arthur.

Summarising the Welsh tradition, we could say that there is no fabulous birth story and no parentage is given. He is generally (but not always) seen as king of all of Britain (meaning of the British people rather than the whole island) with his court at Kelliwic in Cornwall, to which come suitors. These cause the warriors around

Arthur to set forth on adventures, typically to deal with a giant, witch or outsize predator (the beast of Bodmin Moor would be a prime candidate for a modern Arthurian knight!) or perhaps raid the Underworld. He is married, but someone steals his wife away, and he is finally defeated at Camlann.

King lists

Celtic societies set great store by genealogies, and 'king lists' and also family trees were remembered by the bards and frequently recited. Some survive; we are lucky to have one for Dumnonia giving the antecedents of 'Jeudhal, daughter of Theudu son of Peredur son of Cado son of Gereint son of Erbin son of Kynwawr son of Tudwawl' and so on. Such lists can become accidentally inaccurate, or they can be deliberately falsified to 'improve' a claim to the throne. They are also difficult to interpret: is the Gereint here the Geraint whose death at Llongborth is lamented in the Welsh poem? Is Kynwawr 'Cunomorus', which we are told by a Breton writer was King Mark's alternative name?

Geoffrey of Monmouth claimed, in the introduction to his work, that he had access to 'an old book' which had been shown him by Walter of Oxford. This 'old book' has been widely assumed to be a fiction, but Walter was a reputable figure, the Master of Geoffrey's Oxford college, and it seems unlikely that if Geoffrey was engaged in fraud he would have involved this distinguished man. Probably some book did exist, and it may have been a king list preserved in Brittany.

The candidates to be `Arthur'

Every writer about Arthur comes up with a different character, often in differing parts of the country. It is now time to take a brief look at the credentials of some of the candidates. Firstly, there are a few historical figures actually named Arthur.

`Arthur' is widely presumed to be a version of the quite uncommon Roman name Artorius. There was an Artorius Justus in Britain in the third century, and L. Artorius Castus took a legion from York in AD 184 to quell a revolt in Brittany. Arthur could have been descended from either of these, or `Arthur' could be a nickname given him as a result of exploits of his own in Gaul.

In the sixth century a number of rulers named their children Arthur. This is generally assumed to reflect the postumous fame of `King Arthur', but could have had some other cause. The reference in the Gododdin poem in particular could be to one of these later Arthurs. There are at least four of them: Arturius, son of Aedan mac Gabrain of Dalriada; Arthur son of Bicoir the Briton, who slew Mongan mac Fiachna of Ulster; an Arthur whose grandson Feradach signed as witness to a law in Dalriada; and Arthur son of Pedr, prince of Dyfed, born around 575. The son of Aedan is favoured by the Arthurian scholar Richard Barber as his Arthur candidate, but as Aedan was called by the Welsh `Aedan the Treacherous', it seems unlikely that they made his son a super-hero.

Riothamus (a title, not a personal name) is now suggested by Geoffrey Ashe as part at least of the inspiration of the Arthur legend, particularly the Breton tradition on which Geoffrey of Monmouth drew. Certainly his invasion of France and disappearance rather than death, near Avallon, point in that direction. However, if he had already been successful enough against the Saxons to risk taking an army to Gaul in 468, it seems unlikely that he was still militarily active by the time of Badon, perhaps around 500, let alone at Camlann twenty years later. This has to be explained either by saying that Badon was another man's victory, or that Badon actually occurred earlier, say around 480 (which is not impossible but does present some problems) or else that the Arthur of legend was a composite figure (which is quite probable).

However, in his *Les Origines de la Bretagne*, Léon Fleuriot looks at Riothamus from a Breton perspective and makes a convincing case for Riothamus having been not Arthur but Ambrosius Aurelianus making a continental foray. In a continental list of the `kings of the Romans', Ambrosius Aurelianus is described as `king of the Franks and of the Armorican Britons'. This suggests a temporary victory over the Franks (since the Britons never conquered the Franks) and either a kingdom on both sides of the Channel, or else that it was Ambrosius Aurelianus who led the main emigration and transferred his kingdom from Britain to Armorica. Neither is unlikely.

Fleuriot also quotes a later Gallic triad, the `three dishonoured men', of whom the second is Gwrtheyrn [i.e. Vortigern]

> the skinny man who first gave land in that island to the Saxons and who first consorted with them, and who killed by treason Constantine the Small, son of Constantine the Blessed, and exiled the brothers Emrys [Ambrosius] the lord of that land and Uther Pendragon into Armorica and took by trickery the crown of that kingdom. And in the end Uther and Emrys burned Gwrtheyrn in his castle by the Wye in a single burning to avenge their brother.

This would make Arthur, if indeed he was the son of Uther, the nephew of Ambrosius Aurelianus, and gives a plausible succession of Ambrosius-Uther-Arthur.

An ingenious but surely fanciful argument is made in *King Arthur, the True Story* by G Phillips and Martin Keatman for `Arthur' to be not a Roman name but a nickname of one Owain Ddantgwyn. This version involves a combined kingdom of Gwynedd and Powys (which then included much of the English midlands); such a kingdom (if it ever existed) would have dominated Celtic Britain at the time, and its king could have become high king of Britain. The authors derive `Arthur' from the British and Latin words for `bear' (*arth* and *ursus*) thus symbolising Owain's attempt to unify the pro-Roman and nationalist factions in British society. If you believe that you'll believe anything, but it's a good read.

Many theories of Arthur do not give him other names, but assign him different roles. The most common are either as the king of a British kingdom (any one of a dozen or so kingdoms, ranging from Dumnonia to Gloucestershire to Strathclyde) who may have become the dominant king of Britain with some degree of power over a loose federation. Alternatively he may not have been a king, but just a brilliant war leader, probably from a princely family since commoners never had a chance to become leaders.

Arthur's victories are also variously described as anything from local skirmishes clearing small areas of country in which the Saxons tried to settle, to a massive reconquest of the whole of Britain. It is generally agreed that he would have used a small force of armoured cavalry, in a style characteristic of the late Roman empire, giving him the advantage of mobility compared to the Saxons who fought on foot. There is disagreement on whether such soldiers would have fought on horseback or dismounted, since it is generally assumed that the stirrup had not reached Britain, and without stirrups a cavalryman has difficulty striking either with a lance or sword without being knocked from his horse by the blow.

The Saxons always fought on foot, and were still doing so at Hastings. A small British cavalry force could have won many battles, but would have found it hard to consolidate their victory.

Britain in AD 500

Whilst it is impossible to pin down Arthur the person, it is possible to say something about Britain at the time we suppose he lived. It is natural with hindsight to talk in terms of Saxons versus Britons but the politics of the time were more complex than that. The `Saxons' were sub-divided by Bede into Angles, Saxons and Jutes, but they seem also to have included Frisians and many other minor groups. They could probably understand one another's speech, but they were far from united. They had arrived in separate groups and they formed separate and rival kingdoms, sometimes at war with one another. Some of these kingdoms may have contained only Germanic people; others such as Kent or the later Wessex had Saxon overlords but the people were still mostly Britons, perhaps treated as an underclass. The Saxon lords had simply taken over when the Roman (or Gallo-Roman or Romano-British) landowners had departed. It is quite possible that life for some of the serfs actually improved when the Saxons arrived, since the burden of taxes to support distant courts and armies was taken away.

The area held by the Saxons can be roughly marked in modern terms by a line south from the Humber following the motorways M18 and M1 to London. The Saxons dominated almost everywhere east of that line, and also in north and east Kent. The exceptions were the Fens, partially drained by the Romans but flooded again from about AD 200 and inaccessible and unattractive to the Saxons, and a long thin area between London and Cambridge, roughly between the present A10 and A11, which seems to have held out against them. The Saxons also controlled pockets around Southampton and in Sussex. Some of their earliest settlements were in the upper Thames valley, although who controlled it politically is hard to determine.

The British were equally divided. Their small kingdoms with capitals from Exeter to Dumbarton and Edinburgh were often at loggerheads, frequently disputing overlordship. They were quite capable of following Roman tradition and employing Saxon mercenaries against each other, but more often their kings acted like the later feudal barons, supporting their own war-bands of `knights' in the most generous and hospitable manner possible. Early Welsh laws actually make an annual raiding party against a neighbouring state incumbent on the king who, however, had the right to decide which neighbour to attack! Probably it was possible for two neighbouring war-bands to go cattle rustling in the others' lands without ever encountering each other. This was great fun and profitable for everybody except the peasants whose farms were ruined.

A small number of powerful men attempted to retain Roman styles and customs, and even the Latin language, though increasingly that was the preserve of churchmen. There was some respect still for the old ways, but more in word than deed. Roman names were still in use, with British versions: Cei (`Sir Kay') for example was probably Caius and there were several men called Mark – Caius and Marcus being the commonest Roman personal names.

A few of the cities still functioned, particularly Verulamium. This civitas in the Chilterns remained a bastion even when surrounded by Saxons; London was possibly still functioning, and Wroxeter is known to have had new wooden buildings. Many other Roman towns were excavated before archaeological techniques could identify wooden structures; the upper archaeological levels which might have contained post holes have been destroyed, so the extent of urban life there will probably never now be known. However, since there was no money in circulation, trade must have remained on a small scale and for the most part local. One notable exception is Mediterranean wine, which seems to have been imported for court use in substantial quantities.

It is also clear that the Saxons did not destroy the towns. Whereas the destruction of Colchester and Verulamium during Boudicca's revolt was clearly seen by the excavators, there is minimal evidence of such destruction in the fifth century. The main use of the towns in AD 500 was probably for administration and barracks; with a reduced civilian population, the length of the walls was too great for defence. During the fifth century, many towns seem to have been systematically abandoned, with buildings taken down for re-erection elsewhere. Some of the hill forts unused for 400 years were re-occupied with refurbished defences.

The best known of these is South Cadbury, half a mile south of the A303 four miles west of Wincanton, and in consequence an excellent place for a stop and a stroll on the drive from Cornwall to London! It is a most attractive spot, and is still a prime candidate for the site of Arthur's capital, although nothing can be proved. Certainly its fifth century defences are on a massive scale, and there is evidence of large wooden buildings within the camp.

What must life have been like at this time for the peasants in British controlled areas? The whole cost of the war-bands, the ostentatious present-giving, feasting and wine-drinking and the expensive maintenance and breeding of war-horses on the best grazing land all fell upon the peasants. There was often anarchy in the countryside, with British raiding parties as well as occasional raids from the Saxons in the east; the Irish were feared along the west coast, and the Scots from Dalriada and Picts from northern Scotland raided on the northern frontier and the Yorkshire coast, for the Picts were no mean sailors. There were plagues as well, no doubt as a result of a constant state of malnutrition and poverty. In the tales, Arthur and his court make merry every Easter and Christmas – but was there good government and prosperity for all? The view we have inherited is that of the Welsh bards and their Norman equivalents, which is the view of their rich and powerful patrons, that peasants exist to provide for the aristocracy.

Monasteries represented an increasingly popular line of escape from the brutishness of life. Boys as young as five years old might be put into the monastery and scarcely leave it all their lives; it is hardly surprising if monks were sometimes narrow-minded or naive when they wrote the lives of the saints! But by no means all churchmen were men of peace. St Germanus was a muscular Christian who, on his visit in 429, in circumstances far from clear, led an army into battle: they all had to be baptised first, and terrified the enemy by loud shouts of alleluya. One is reminded of the Chinese Christian general at the time of the Boxer rebellion who baptised his army with a fire hose. (Bede, incidentally describes Germanus as *dux belli*, a title almost identical to *dux bellorum*.) For most of its inhabitants, Britain in AD500 was a pretty miserable place.

The major Arthurian sites

Tintagel: Until recently Tintagel was scorned by Arthur scholars, but now it is recognised as a major sixth century site, probably used as a royal court in the summer months. See pages 8-9.

Badon: The siege of Badon Hill was a great British victory over `the Saxons' and brought the Britons external peace for nearly a generation. They seem to have used the time to settle old scores between themselves, bringing about the ultimate loss of their country. It is not known when this battle was fought, and there are two schools of thought on where 'Badon' was.

Nennius says it was *in monte Badonis*, 'on the hill of Bado'. (Latin names change at the end for grammatical purposes, and we can infer the name Bado from Nennius' phrase.) Gildas refers to it as the siege of *mons Badonicus*, 'the Bado hill'. One school of thought has looked for places called Badbury, and there are five, spread from Dorset to Lincolnshire, most of them with an iron age earthwork in the vicinity. The other and, to my mind, more likely option is that Bado is Bath. In Roman times it was known as Aquae Sulis, the waters of Sul, but in Welsh it is Caerfaddon, *caer* meaning 'city', *faddon* meaning 'of Baddon'. (Where Latin made its grammatical changes at the end of the word, Celtic languages make the change at the beginning.) The word Baddon (pronounced bathon) may have imitated the Saxon Bathonea or it may have preceded it.

Bath is a strategically likely site for such a battle. Indeed the truly decisive battle won by the Saxons in 577 was only five miles north at Dyrham, and a major battle in the Civil War was fought on Lansdowne, which could reasonably be called 'the hill of Bath'.

As always in this story, it is impossible to be sure. The medieval Latin word *bado* was slang for 'I stand and gawp' – irrelevant but not entirely inappropriate!

Camelot: Probably totally mythical, and placed by medieval writers wherever pleased their audience best: but the Welsh tradition placed Arthur's court at `Kelliwic' in Cornwall, which has been tentatively identified with Killibury hill fort, two miles north-east of Wadebridge. For South Cadbury, see page 28.

Glastonbury: Supposedly the place of Arthur and Guinevere's burial, Glastonbury is certainly a very ancient religious site. It seems probable that it was a pagan site converted to Christian use in pre-Saxon times, and the Abbey records in the early twelfth century included a charter granted by a king of Dumnonia. It was not uncommon for important lay persons to be buried within a monastic site in Christian Celtic society so Arthur might have been buried there. Against this, there was a powerful tradition in Cornwall and Brittany that Arthur was not dead at all, but would return in the hour of need; and the Welsh and Cornish, as well as Geoffrey of Monmouth, insisted that Arthur's grave was unknown.

Arthur's connection with Glastonbury before 1190 consists of one story, written down about 1125, in which Arthur besieged Melwas (a Somerset chieftain who had abducted Guinevere) bringing his army from Devon and Cornwall for the purpose. William of Malmesbury conducted an intensive examination of the abbey records but found nothing about Arthur there. And then suddenly in 1191, at Henry II's prompting, the monks decided to dig in their grounds and found, or seemed to find, the graves of Arthur and Guinevere, his bones being of great size and hers being of great beauty – whatever that implies!

This was of great use to the abbey, which gained an additional tourist attraction (for pilgrimages then fulfilled the same functions as holidays now) and pleased the king, who was able to show the tiresome Cornish, Welsh and Bretons (then within Henry's empire) that King Arthur really *was* dead and would not rise again to rescue them from the Anglo-Normans. It was extremely convenient all round. From that time, but not before, the isle of Glastonbury became identified as the Isle of Avalon.

If the discovery of Arthur's burial was a faked job, it would not be out of character for medieval monks, who not infrequently forged charters or produced miracle-working statues. One mysterious point, however, was a leaden cross said to have been found within the coffin. Several writers described the cross at the time, failing to agree on the precise wording of its inscription, but in 1607 the antiquary Camden illustrated a cross which was then shown at Glastonbury, presumably but not certainly the one which was exhumed in 1191. The lettering he records is

HIC IACET SEPULTUS INCLITUS REX ARTURIUS
IN INSULA AVALONI
'Here lies buried the famous King Arthur, in the Isle of Avalon'

The lettering style appears to indicate the tenth or eleventh century, which tallies neither with a sixth century genuine burial nor with a twelfth century fake, unless the monks were trying to use ye olde worlde lettering. It is at least possible that the burial had been accidentally dug up in the mid-tenth century when the abbot, St Dunstan, is known to have had work done in the same area of the abbey. Believing, on good or bad grounds, that they had found King Arthur's grave, he might have had a commemorative cross made before reinterring the coffin.

Camlann: The scene of the final and fatal battle has been as much argued over as has Badon. Cornish tradition and Geoffrey of Monmouth place it at Slaughter Bridge over the River Camel a mile or so north of Camelford. This may be the scene of a later battle, when the Saxons were invading Cornwall in AD825, which could have given rise to a mistaken tradition. The main route into Cornwall until the later middle ages was by way of Camelford and Wadebridge, which makes Slaughter Bridge a tactically likely place. After the battle, Sir Bedivere reluctantly threw King Arthur's sword into a lake, which is (without a shred of evidence) indentified as Dozmary Pool, near Jamaica Inn.

The words *cam lann* mean 'crooked glen' so there are plenty of alternative sites in Britain! Etymologically the Roman fort of 'Camboglanna' on Hadrian's Wall is a strong contender, and if Arthur was a national leader we should not be surprised to find him fighting anywhere in the country.

The Tristan and Iseult story: Although part of the traditional group of stories associated with Arthur, this story almost certainly is of quite independent origin. Ironically it has references to Cornish places which can be quite positively identified, unlike any of the Arthurian sites (except Tintagel and Dimelioc). King Mark's castle was at Castle Dore, an iron age earthwork near Fowey reoccupied in the post-Roman period. Probably the fort was used only in times of danger, and Mark's palace was at Lantyan, or perhaps more specifically at a settlement called 'Castle', a mile or so south of Lostwithiel on the west side of the River Fowey. A standing stone now by the road just outside Fowey is said (for the lettering is now too worn to read) to commemorate 'Drustanus son of Cunomorus' Celticised, the names are Drust, or Tristan, son of Cynfawr. Since there was a historical Breton King Mark who was also known as Cunomorus, the stone has been accepted with perhaps a spot of wishful thinking as the memorial stone of Tristan himself; the most we can say, is that it is by no means impossible.

In Beroul's version of the story, we also find St Sampson's church (Golant), St Sampson's island (probably a river sandbank near Golant), the Forest of Morresk (the triangle between the A39 and the Truro and Tresillian Rivers, though probably a very much larger forest in Tristan's time) and a ford at Malpas near Truro. Tristan's Leap is traditionally placed at Chapel Rock, Mevagissey, but this seems too far from where the story is centered. And it is of course possible that Beroul knew Cornwall and simply chose to place the events in real locations to give some local colour.

For some thousand years people have been trying to pin down exact locations for Arthur and his literary companions, on evidence totally inadequate. It is not surprising if sometimes invented or fanciful connections have been taken by later generations to be reliable facts. But at the very least, to explore Arthur and Tristan's Cornwall is no dafter than to explore Hardy's Wessex!

For what it is worth, my own diffident view after two years research is that Arthur most probably *did* exist; that he was a successful young warrior related to Ambrosius Aurelianus (perhaps a nephew, possibly an illegitimate son of Uther) who became king of a territory in the south-west, perhaps stretching from Cornwall to the Mendips, and that with the temporary support of the other British kingdoms he fought successfully for the national cause as far afield as Lincolnshire and Scotland. But after Badon, all semblance of British unity disappeared. Arthur may have tried to retain Roman values in the face of increasing barbarism and religious bigotry, or he may have been just another aristocratic freebooter. For whatever reason, he was not universally popular, and he died in a civil war. His actual achievements were in no way proportionate to his inspirational effect over the next 1500 years.